THE *Golf Doctor*

THE Golf Doctor

Robin McMillan
and John Andrisani

Illustrations by Ken Lewis

BARNES
&NOBLE
BOOKS
NEW YORK

2000 Barnes & Noble Books

ISBN 0-7607-2018-5

Printed and bound in the United States of America

00 01 02 03 MP 9 8 7 6 5 4 3 2 1

QW

FOR DANBY

ACKNOWLEDGMENTS

We would like to thank our editor, Peter Gethers, for his contributions to this book.

We also want to acknowledge the special contributions of Mickey Robinson, whose marketing insights and erratic short game helped shape this project.

TABLE OF CONTENTS

1   The Rules of Golf Simplified

10

1 The Rules of Golf Simplified

The Rules of Golf are complex and can often be confusing. While it would be impossible to condense the entire 128 pages of the Official Rules of Golf (and the 471 pages devoted to "Decisions" on the Rules) into one chapter of this book, the vast majority of rules and situations you will encounter during the course of play can, fortunately, be summarized in a relatively simple and user-friendly fashion. We have been as thorough as possible, but should an unusual situation arise that is not covered here, an official solution can be obtained from the United States Golf Association, which oversees the Rules of Golf. Write to: United States Golf Association, Golf House, Far Hills, N.J. 07931-0708.

CHAPTER CONTENTS:

1 DEFINITIONS
2. THE RULES
3. ETIQUETTE

4. PENALTY STROKES AT A GLANCE

DEFINITIONS

Integral to the Rules of Golf are certain "Definitions" that will help clarify and simplify the Rules themselves. It will be helpful to familiarize yourself with the language of the Definitions before consulting the Rules.

Addressing the Ball

A player has addressed the ball when he has taken his stance and has "grounded" the club— i.e., he has soled the club behind the ball. A player is not allowed to ground a club if his ball is in a hazard.

Bunker

A bunker, often colloquially called a sandtrap, is a hazard consisting of a prepared area from which turf or soil has been removed and replaced with sand or similar material. Any grass that borders the bunker is not part of the hazard.

Casual Water

Casual water is any temporary accumulation of water, often found after a rainstorm or where drainage is poor, that is not part of a water hazard. Dew is not casual water. A player may take "relief" from casual water by dropping his ball within one clublength of the nearest point of relief but no closer to the hole. The way to test for casual water if there is any doubt is to take your stance. If water is visible, you will be entitled to relief. A player is entitled to relief if his ball or his stance is in casual water or if the casual water interferes with his swing.

Fellow Competitor

Another player in your group in stroke-play competition.

Ground Under Repair

This is any part of the course marked GROUND UNDER REPAIR. Material piled for removal or a hole made by a greenkeeper is considered ground under repair, although it does not have to be so marked. A player is entitled to relief from Ground Under Repair.

Hazard
A hazard is any bunker or water hazard.

Honor
The player or team entitled to play first from the teeing ground is said to have the "honor."

Lateral Water Hazard
A lateral water hazard is a water hazard marked by red stakes or lines. An important distinction is made in the Rules between a water hazard and a lateral water hazard, because the latter provides additional procedures for taking relief.

Loose Impediments
These are *natural* objects such as stones, leaves, twigs, or branches that are not fixed or growing, not solidly embedded, nor sticking to the ball. Dew is not a loose impediment. Sand and loose soil are loose impediments only on the putting green.

Obstruction
An obstruction is anything artificial, including the artificial surfaces and sides of roads and paths. Such items as pieces of paper, cigarette ends, or bottle caps are obstructions. Exceptions include out-of-bounds markers, usually white stakes but possibly walls, fences, and railings, and any part of an immovable object that has

been declared an integral part of the course. Trees, bushes, and boulders are not obstructions.

Opponent
An opposing player in match-play competition.

Out of Bounds
Out of bounds is ground on which play is prohibited. It is normally found on the perimeter of a golf course and is marked by white stakes or fence posts. A player may stand out of bounds to play a ball that is within bounds.

Outside Agency
Anything that is not part of a match or, in stroke-play, not part of a competitor's side. A match comprises the players, their equipment, and their caddies or carts. Neither wind nor water is an outside agency. With some exceptions, if a ball is deflected or stopped by an outside agency, no penalty is incurred and the ball should be played as it lies. This is a "rub of the green."

Provisional Ball
When a player believes his ball may be lost or that he has hit it out of bounds, he may play a "provisional" ball. The player should play the provisional until he reaches the place where the original ball is likely to be. If he cannot find the original ball, or if it is out of bounds, the player must take the required stroke-and-distance penalty and continue to play the provisional ball. The provisional ball rule is designed to save time.

Putting Green

The putting green—normally known as "the green"—is any ground on the course specially prepared for putting. A ball is on the putting green when any part of it touches the putting green.

Stance

A player has taken his stance when he has placed both feet in a position to make a stroke.

Stroke

Officially, a stroke is the forward movement of the club to fairly strike at and move the ball. If the ball is swung at, it counts as a stroke.

Teeing Ground

The teeing ground is the starting place for the hole to be played. It is a rectangular area two clublengths deep, the front and sides of which are defined by the outside limits of two tee-markers. The ball must be played from the teeing ground, but the player does not have to take his stance inside the teeing ground to play the ball.

Through the Green

The whole area of the course except for the teeing ground and the putting green of the hole being played, and any hazards.

Water Hazard

Any sea, lake, pond, or ditch (even if it does not contain water), or any other open water course, is considered a water hazard. Water hazards are defined by yellow lines or stakes.

Rules at a Glance

For quick reference, the following is a list of
simplified rules appearing on pages 24 to 44.

General

1. Match Play vs. Stroke Play
2. Number of Golf Clubs
3. Club Specifications
4. Ball Specifications
5. Ball Unfit for Play
6. Asking for, or Giving, Advice

On the Tee

7. Order of Play
8. Teeing Up the Ball
9. Ball Accidentally Knocked off Tee
10. Ball Blown off Tee by Wind
11. Stopping Your Swing in Mid-Stroke
12. Ball Accidentally Hit During Practice Swing
13. Ball Missed Completely
14. Ball Hit out of Bounds
15. Lost Ball

On the Fairway

16. Improving Your Lie
17. The Ball Moves
18. Playing the Wrong Ball
19. Fellow Competitor or Opponent Plays Your Ball
20. Identifying Your Ball
21. Swing Obstructed by Loose Impediments
22. Ball Lying near Stake Interfering with Your Stance or Swing
23. Ball Embedded
24. Ball in a Hole
25. Ball in Divot Hole

The Rules

Note: The following Rules are grouped under six categories for easy reference: General; On the Tee; On the Fairway; In the Rough, or in a Hazard; On the Green; and Etiquette. Neither the categories or the numbered rules correspond to the United States Golf Association's official Rules of Golf. For the purpose of simplification we have included the appropriate Rule in the situation where it most frequently applies.

General

1. Match-Play vs. Stroke-Play
The two basic forms of competitive play are match-play and stroke-play. In match-play the players count the number of strokes and penalty strokes taken on each hole and the hole is won by the player with the lower total. A hole is tied, or "halved," if the opposing players take the same number of strokes. The player who is more holes "up" than there are holes remaining to be played wins the match. In stroke-play (sometimes called "medal play"), players count total strokes per round. The winner is the player who takes the fewest strokes.

Match play can be played in several formats. In a four-ball match, two players play their better ball against the better ball of two other players.

2. Number of Golf Clubs
You are allowed to carry no more than 14 clubs when you start a round or during the course of play. In stroke-play you incur a two-stroke

penalty for every hole you play with more than 14 clubs, up to a maximum of four strokes. In match-play you are penalized a maximum of two holes. The penalty is applied to the state of the match. For example, suppose a player who has lost the first two holes is discovered by his opponent on the third tee to have more than 14 clubs in his bag. The player would be four holes down even though only two holes have been played.

3. Club Specifications
The shaft of a golf club must be straight and more than 18 inches long. Except for putters, the grip must be generally circular in cross-section. The grip must not contain any bulge or waist. The clubhead must be generally plain in shape, with all parts rigid and functional. Appendages for the purpose of aiming are not permitted. The distance between grooves must be at least three times the surface width of a groove.

4. Ball Specifications
A golf ball must not weigh more than 1.62 ounces. Its diameter must not be less than 1.68 inches. A ball can have any number of dimples in any configuration so long as the ball conforms to USGA standards in terms of spherical symmetry, initial velocity, and overall distance.

5. Ball Unfit for Play
A ball that is visibly cut, cracked, or out of shape can be replaced at any time without penalty during play of a hole if the damage

occurred on that hole. A ball that has mud on it, or has had its surface scratched or scraped cannot be considered unfit for play. A player is always allowed to change balls between holes.

6. Asking for, or Giving, Advice

A golfer may ask for advice only from his partner or either of their caddies. You will incur a two-stroke penalty (or lose the hole) if you ask for, or give, advice to an opponent or fellow competitor. However, this only concerns advice about how to make a swing, or advice that may influence a player in selecting a club. Information about the position of hazards, or information on the Rules, is not considered advice.

On the Tee

7. Order of Play

The player who takes the fewest number of strokes on the previous hole is said to have the "honor" and tees off first. If the previous hole was tied or "halved," the last player to win a hole has the honor. In four-ball play, a team may determine which of its two players tees off first. In stroke-play, the player in the group who took the fewest strokes on the previous hole has the honor. When all players have left the teeing ground, the ball farthest from the hole should be played first.

8. Teeing Up the Ball

You may tee your ball anywhere between the two tee-markers and up to two clublengths behind the markers. You do not have to stand in

26

this area to play your shot. You cannot move the tee-markers. You are not required to use a tee on the teeing round.

9. Ball Accidentally Knocked off Tee
A ball is not in play until you have made a stroke from the teeing ground, so you may retee the ball without penalty.

10. Ball Blown off Tee by Wind
If the ball is not yet in play (see No. 9, above), you may retee it.

11. Stopping Your Swing in Mid-Stroke
You may voluntarily stop your swing at any time before the clubhead reaches the ball.

12. Ball Accidentally Hit During Practice Swing
If you hit your ball while taking a practice swing before teeing off, you would not incur a penalty since the ball was not yet in play. Retee your ball and begin again. Once the ball is in play, however, you would pick up one penalty stroke for moving a ball at rest, and must replace your ball.

13. Ball Missed Completely
This counts as one stroke if you intended to hit it.

14. Ball Hit out of Bounds
If you hit a ball out of bounds, you must play again from the same spot, count both strokes and add a penalty stroke. The penalty is known as "stroke and distance." You may retee your ball if the original stroke was a teeshot. If you

are not sure if your ball has come to rest out of bounds, you may play a provisional ball.

15. Lost Ball

If you suspect your ball may be lost, you may hit a provisional ball. You are allowed five minutes to search for the original ball. If you cannot find it, the provisional ball becomes the ball in play and you incur a stroke-and-distance penalty. Many players drop another ball and play it from where they think the ball was lost, but this is illegal. A player must play again from where the previous shot was played. The purpose of hitting the provisional ball is to avoid an unnecessary waste of time.

On the Fairway

16. Improving Your Lie

You may not improve your lie anywhere. Improving your lie carries a two-stroke penalty (or loss of hole). However, if underfoot conditions are poor, many clubs invoke "winter rules," and players may opt to take "preferred lies." The USGA does not recognize "winter rules."

17. The Ball Moves

If your ball moves after you have addressed it — i.e., after you've taken your stance and have grounded your club — you are deemed to have moved it and must count a penalty stroke and replace the ball. If, however, it moves after you have begun your swing and you do not stop your swing, you must count the stroke, add a penalty stroke, and play your ball as it lies.

An exception: If your ball moves after you have addressed it but returns to its original position, no penalty is incurred.

18. Playing the Wrong Ball
Playing the wrong ball incurs two penalty strokes (or loss of hole). In stroke-play, rectify your mistake immediately. If you do not rectify before playing from the teeing ground of the next hole, or if you leave the green on the final hole, you will be subject to disqualification in stroke-play. If two competitors play each other's balls, each would be subject to a two-stroke penalty. In match-play, the player who erred first would lose the hole.

Note: There is no penalty for playing a wrong ball in a hazard. In this instance, you should return to the hazard and play the correct ball.

19. Fellow Competitor or Opponent Plays Your Ball
Notify the other player, who must add two penalty strokes (or lose the hole). You should then play your ball from as close as possible to the original lie.

20. Identifying Your Ball
To identify your ball you can mark the ball's position and lift it and identify it (after advising your opponent or fellow competitor of your intention). If you have to clean your ball to identify it, clean away only as much as is necessary for identification. You are not allowed to do this in a hazard, but there is no penalty for playing a wrong ball in a hazard.

21. Swing Obstructed by Loose Impediments

You may move twigs, rocks that are not solidly embedded, leaves, or other loose natural objects anywhere on the golf course except when both the ball and the natural object lie in a hazard. Except on the green, if your ball moves after you have touched loose impediments within one clublength of it, and before you have addressed it, you incur a one-stroke penalty. Return the ball to its original position. If the movement occurs after you have begun the backward motion of your swing and you do not discontinue your swing, you must count the stroke, add a penalty stroke, and play your ball as it lies.

22. Ball Lying near Stake Interfering with Stance or Swing

If it is a hazard stake (red or yellow) you may move the stake to make your shot. (If you have to remove it completely, make sure you replace it.) If it's an out-of-bounds stake (white) you may not move the stake. Removing an out-of-bounds stake carries a two-stroke penalty (or loss of hole).

23. Ball Embedded

On the fairway, you can dig your ball out, clean it, and drop it as close as possible to where it embedded, but no closer to the hole. A ball that embeds in the rough has to be played as it lies, or declared unplayable, unless a Local Rule says otherwise.

24. Ball in a Hole
Relief is awarded without penalty from any hole made by a burrowing animal, which includes rabbits, moles, groundhogs, gophers, etc. (Dogs do not count as "burrowing animals.")

25. Ball in Divot Hole
Play your ball as it lies.

26. Ball on Cart Path
A cart path is an immovable obstruction and you are therefore entitled to relief. Mark the nearest "point of relief"—i.e., off the cart path but not nearer the hole—by pushing a tee into the ground at that point, and drop your ball within one clublength of the tee, no closer to the hole.

If your ball is not on a cart path, but is near enough to it so that you must stand on the path in order to swing, you are entitled to the same relief as if your ball were on the path.

27. Rules for Dropping a Ball
Hold the ball at arm's length, your arm horizontal to the ground, and let it go. Your ball must be dropped where the relevant Rule requires it to be dropped. If the ball rolls more than two clublengths from where it hit the ground, drop it again. If the ball rolls such a distance a second time, you must place the ball on the spot at which the ball hit the ground when you last dropped it.

28. Ball Hitting a Golf Cart
This is one of the more unusual rules. If your ball hits your golf cart, or your partner's, you will incur a two-stroke penalty and must play your ball as it lies (in match-play you would lose the hole). If you hit your opponent's cart in match-play, you incur no penalty and may either play the ball as it lies or cancel the stroke and replay the shot without penalty. If you hit another player's cart in stroke-play, you must count the stroke and play the ball as it lies without penalty.

In the Rough, or in a Hazard

29. Loose Impediments Obstructing Swing
You may move loose impediments anywhere on the golf course except when the ball and the impediment lie in a hazard.

30. Rules Governing the Rough
If a bush or branches of a tree interfere with your stance or swing, you can move them as much as is necessary to fairly take your stance. You can move any branches, leaves, or similar obstructions if they are not fixed or growing (as such they are considered "loose impediments"). In long grass, you may not flatten the grass around your ball.

31. Unplayable Lie
When you cannot swing at the ball, you can declare your ball unplayable. Then, under a one-stroke penalty, you may: (a) play again from the spot where the previous stroke was played, counting both strokes; (b) drop your ball within

two clublengths of the ball's unplayable location, no closer to the hole; or (c) drop your ball back on the extension of an imaginary line running from the hole through the unplayable location. (See Figure 1.1.)

A ball may not be declared unplayable if it is in a water hazard or lateral water hazard. You should proceed under the Rule governing those hazards. If you declare your ball unplayable in a bunker and you elect to proceed under (b) or (c) above, it must be dropped in the bunker. In any case, you may clean an unplayable ball before proceeding.

32. Ball in Tree
If you cannot identify your ball, it is lost. If you can identify it, you may play it as it lies but you cannot "build a stance"—i.e., stand on a bench. If you can identify the ball but cannot play it, you must declare it unplayable.

33. Rules Governing Water Hazards
It is not just the water that is part of a water hazard; it is everything inside the boundary of the hazard. Your ball may be in a water hazard but not in water within the hazard. Do not ground your club or remove loose impediments from inside the hazard. Both actions carry two-stroke penalties (or loss of hole).

If you hit into a water hazard you have several options, depending on whether you have hit into a water hazard or a lateral water hazard. A water hazard is defined by yellow stakes or lines, a lateral water hazard by red stakes or lines.

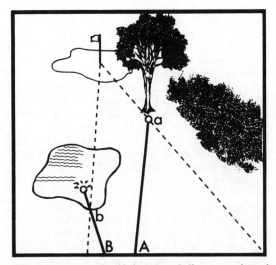

Figure 1.1 For an unplayable lie (A) or a ball in a water hazard (B), one option is to drop the ball back on the extension of an imaginary line from the hole through the point of the unplayable lie (a) or through the point the ball last crossed the margin of the water hazard (b).

If you hit into a water hazard you may: (a) play your ball as it lies; (b) play again from the spot where the previous stroke was played, count both strokes and add a penalty stroke (stroke and distance); or (c) drop a ball on the extension of an imaginary line drawn from the hole through the point at which the ball last crossed the margin of the hazard and add a penalty stroke (see Figure 1.1.).

If you hit into a lateral water hazard, you have two additional options. You may: (d) drop your ball within two clublengths of the point at which your ball last crossed the hazard margin, but no closer to the hole, and add a penalty stroke or (e) drop your ball within two clublengths of a point on the *opposite* side of the hazard equidistant from the hole (where a better lie or a less obstructed shot may await you) and add a penalty stroke.

The penalty for not following one of the above procedures is two strokes (or loss of hole).

34. Ball on Edge of Water Hazard

If any part of your ball comes to rest on the line defining the hazard, then it is considered to be in the hazard, as the line is part of the hazard. This is not the case with balls hit out of bounds. The whole ball has to be out of bounds for you to incur any penalty.

35. Loose Impediments in a Bunker

Twigs, stones, leaves, or any other "loose impediments" may not be touched when both the ball and the impediment lie in a hazard. The penalty is two strokes (or loss of hole). You may, however, move objects that are not loose impediments—i.e., unnatural objects such as cigarette butts, tin cans, bottles, papers, etc.

36. Touching the Sand in a Bunker

A bunker is a hazard. You may not ground your club in a hazard before you hit out of the hazard. The penalty is two strokes (or loss of hole).

37. Ball Completely Buried in a Bunker

You must play the ball as it lies or declare it unplayable. If you cannot see it, you may brush away only enough sand to be able to see a part of the ball.

38. Ball in Bunker Obstructed by Rake

A rake is a movable obstruction no matter where it lies. If your ball moves while the rake is being moved, replace the ball without penalty. If your ball comes to rest *on* the rake, you may lift the ball, move the rake, and drop your ball as close as possible to its original position.

On the Green

39. Hitting onto Wrong Green

Never play your ball from the wrong green. Establish your nearest point of relief (the nearest part of the course off the green, no closer to the hole), and drop within one clublength of that point, no closer to the hole. There is no penalty.

40. Ball Hitting the Flagstick

If your approach shot hits the flagstick, or if your ball hits the flagstick when you are putting from off the green, there is no penalty if the flagstick is unattended, and you should play the ball as it lies. If your ball hits the flagstick while you are putting on the green, whether or not it is attended, you incur two penalty strokes (or loss of hole).

41. Putting from off the Green
A putt from off the green should be treated as any other approach shot. You may remove any loose impediments from the green and repair ball marks (on the green) before hitting.

42. Ball Lodged Against Flagstick
A ball is not considered holed until all of it is below the level of the lip of the hole. In such a case, you may remove the flagstick. If your ball falls into the hole, you are deemed to have holed it with your last stroke. If it does not fall in, and is moved when the flagstick is removed, you must place the ball on the edge of the hole without penalty.

43. Loose Impediments on Putting Line
Sand, soil, or other loose impediments on your putting line may be picked up or brushed away with your hand or a club. Dew is not a loose impediment.

If your ball moves due to removal of a loose impediment, replace your ball without penalty.

44. Ball Overhanging Lip of Hole
You should approach your ball without unreasonable delay. You may then wait 10 seconds for the ball to fall in. If the ball falls in after 10 seconds have expired, you earn a penalty stroke, i.e., the same score that you would have had if you had tapped the ball into the cup from the lip.

45. Hitting Another Ball While Putting on the Green

In match-play, if your ball hits another ball, including your partner's, while putting on the green, the other ball must be replaced and you must play your ball as it lies with no penalty. In stroke-play, you would incur a two-stroke penalty, and the ball that was moved must be replaced.

46. Hitting Other Objects While Putting

If your ball hits your opponent, his caddie, or equipment in match-play, you may play the ball as it lies without penalty or elect to replay the stroke, provided no other player on either side has made a stroke since your original stroke. If you hit a fellow competitor, his caddie, or equipment in stroke-play, you must count the stroke and play the ball as it lies without penalty.

47. Spike Marks on Line of Putt

Fixing spike marks on your line carries a two-stroke penalty (or loss of hole). You should repair them before you leave the green, however.

You may repair ballmarks—i.e., impressions made by a ball landing on the putting green.

48. Marking Your Ball

If you are marking the position of a ball to take relief, it's best to use a tee. If you are marking the position of a ball on a putting green, use a plastic marker (they can usually be found in pro shops or locker rooms) or a small coin. It is recommended that you place your marker just behind the ball. If your mark is on another player's putting line, line up the putter with an object off the green and replace the marker the length of a putter's head from your ball's position. Always replace your ball in its original position.

49. Cleaning Your Ball

You may clean your ball on the putting green. You may also clean your ball when identifying it (clean only as much as allows you to identify it) and any time you lift the ball except: (a) when you are determining that your ball is unfit for play or (b) when you have lifted it because it is interfering with or assisting someone else's play. If you clean your ball illegally, you incur a one-stroke penalty.

ETIQUETTE

Golf etiquette is such an integral part of the game that it is the first entry found in the official Rules of Golf.

- Do not move, talk, or stand close to a player or directly behind the ball or hole when a player is making a stroke.
- Be ready to play when it is your turn.
- Do not play until those playing in front of you are out of range.
- When searching for a ball that may be lost, wave those playing behind you through.
- Allow faster and/or smaller groups to play through.
- Leave the putting green as soon as a hole is completed.
- Wait until you would not be delaying play to mark any scorecards.
- Rake sand smooth after hitting out of a bunker.
- Repair any ball impression marks on a green—not just your own.
- Repair any spike marks on a green when your group has finished putting (it is illegal to repair spike marks to improve your line).
- Repair or replace your divots.
- Mind where you lay your golf bag down. Do not lay it on the putting green.
- Do not park golf cars or carts close to the green.
- Make sure the flagstick has been properly placed in the hole before leaving the green.
- Do not damage the course during a practice swing.
- If at all possible, do not take a practice swing. It delays play.

- Do not spend a great amount of time working out yardages.
- Be sure to shout *"Fore"* if you at all suspect that your ball may be in danger of hitting someone.
- Be courteous to those in your group and anyone else on the course.

PENALTY STROKES AT A GLANCE (Most Common Infractions)

These are general penalties. The penalty may be different depending on the situation you encounter.

Loss of Hole (Match-Play)
- Carrying excess clubs.
- Asking advice from, or giving advice to, opponent during a round.
- Placing an object to indicate line of play and leaving it there when stroke is being played.
- Improving the lie of the ball, the area of intended swing, or the line of play.
- Removing boundary stake interfering with swing.
- Building a stance.
- Touching ground in a hazard or water in a water hazard when the ball lies in the hazard.
- Touching or moving a loose impediment in a hazard when the ball lies in the hazard.
- Playing a moving ball.
- Playing wrong ball, except in a hazard.
- Standing astride or on line of putt while making a stroke.
- Ball striking attended flagstick.
- Player's ball deflected or stopped by himself, his partner, or either of their caddies or equipment.
- Playing ball dropped or placed in wrong place.

Two Strokes (Stroke-Play)
- Carrying excess clubs.

- Asking for advice from, or giving advice to, opponent or fellow competitor during round.
- Placing an object to indicate line of play and leaving it there while making a stroke.
- Playing from outside the teeing ground.
- Improving lie of ball, area of intended swing, or line of play.
- Removing white boundary stake that interferes with swing.
- Building a stance.
- Touching ground in a hazard or water in a water hazard when the ball lies in the hazard.
- Touching or moving loose impediments in a hazard when the ball lies in the hazard.
- Playing a moving ball.
- Playing a wrong ball, except in a hazard.
- Standing astride or on line of putt while making a stroke.
- Ball striking attended flagstick or attendant.
- Player's ball deflected or stopped by himself, his partner, or either of their caddies or equipment.
- Playing ball dropped or placed in wrong place.

One Stroke

- Not telling opponent or fellow competitor you are about to lift ball to see if it is unfit for play or to identify it.
- Striking the ball more than once while making a stroke.
- Ball in play moving after address.
- Cleaning ball when not permitted.
- Ball lost or out of bounds (stroke and distance).

- Taking relief for an unplayable ball.
- Taking relief for ball in water hazard.

Disqualification
- Agreeing to waive rules.
- Failing to hole out before playing from next teeing ground (stroke-play only).
- Purposely changing playing characteristics of a club during round.
- Applying foreign material to clubface or ball.
- Using illegal ball.
- Returning score for hole lower than actually taken (stroke-play only).
- Playing from outside teeing ground and not rectifying error (stroke-play only).
- Using artificial devices.
- Playing wrong ball and not rectifying error (stroke-play only).

AUTHOR'S NOTE

Chapters 2 through 7 comprise the instruction section of this book. Please note that all instruction is for right-hand golfers. Left-hand golfers must reverse left and right designations.

2 Basic Shotmaking

Much of golf instruction is based on how the shot you want to hit differs from the "norm." It is helpful to refamiliarize yourself with what constitutes the setup and instructions for hitting golf's basic shots. The following are simple tips on grip, stance, ball position, clubface alignment, swing path, and the ten basic shots of golf.

BASIC SHOTMAKING AT A GLANCE

THE BASIC SETUP
1. Grip
2. Stance
3. Ball Position
4. Clubface Alignment
5. Swing Path

THE BASIC SHOTS
1. The Drive
2. The Fairway Wood
3. The Long Iron
4. The Medium Iron
5. The Short Iron
6. The Pitching Wedge
7. The Pitch-and-Run
8. The Chip
9. The Bunker Shot
10. The Putt

The Basic Setup

1. The Grip (Figure 2.1)

Ninety-five percent of all Tour pros use the *Vardon* or *overlapping* grip (pinky of the right hand overlaps the forefinger of the left hand). Whether you choose to play with the Vardon grip, the *interlock* (pinky of right hand hooks together with the forefinger of the left hand), or the *baseball* type, *full-finger* grip (all ten fingers hold the club's handle), when hitting a straight shot each of the V's formed by the thumb and

Figure 2.1 The Grip

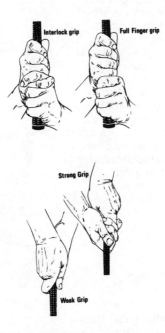

Interlock grip Full Finger grip

Strong Grip

Weak Grip

forefinger of each hand should point midway
between your right shoulder and your chin.
When hitting a left-to-right shot, turn both of
your hands a little toward the target—in a
"weak" position. To turn the ball from right to
left, turn your hands a bit away from the
target—in a "strong" position.

49

2. The Stance (Figure 2.2)

Square (for straight shots): feet are lined up parallel to a line running from the ball to the target; *open* (for fades): front foot is moved back away from the ball and an imaginary line drawn to touch the tips of your shoes would run away from the target line; *closed* (for draws): front foot is moved closer to the ball, and an imaginary line drawn to touch the tips of your shoes would run toward (and then across) the target line.

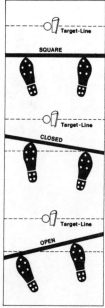

Figure 2.2 The Stance

3. Ball Position (Figure 2.3)

There are two schools of thought for positioning the ball in the stance. Many pros, Jack Nicklaus for one, play all shots off their left heel. Most others believe you should play the driver off the left heel and move the ball slightly back progressively as you swing more lofted clubs (but no farther back than the mid-point of your stance). Experiment to find what works best for you.

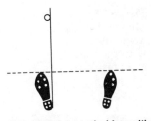

The most popular method for positioning the ball

Figure 2.3 Ball Position. Play all shots off your left heel *or* play the drives off your left heel; then, as the loft of the clubface increases, gradually move the ball back toward the mid-point of your stance. Experiment to see what method works best for you.

4. Clubface Alignment (Figure 2.4)

(a) Square clubface alignment: clubface is aimed directly at target; (b) open clubface alignment: clubface is aimed to the right of target; (c) Closed clubface alignment: clubface is aimed to the left of the target.

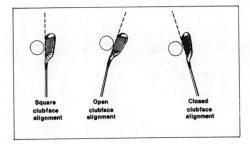

Square clubface alignment   Open clubface alignment   Closed clubface alignment

Figure 2.4 Clubface Alignment

5. Swing Path (Figure 2.5)
The route the clubhead takes
relative to the target line
varies according to the shot
you are playing: (a) inside-

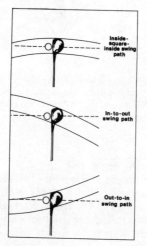

Figure 2.5 Swing Path

square-inside swing path: for "straight" shots;
(b) in-out swing path: for draws; (c) out-to-in
swing path: for fades.

THE BASIC SHOTS

1. The Drive
Tee the ball so that half of the ball is above the top of the clubface. Position the ball off your left heel. Think tempo.

2. The Fairway Wood
Play the ball about a ball's width behind your front heel, with a slightly narrower stance than for a drive. (This type of stance promotes a downward hit that imparts backspin on the ball.) Do not try to "sweep" the ball but hit down on it as you would a medium iron (i.e., a 5- or 6-iron).

3. The Long Iron (Figure 2.6)
Play the ball a couple of inches behind your front heel. (This forward position allows the club to stay low to the ground through impact, making for a sweeping action in the hitting area. Make a good hip turn on the backswing and then swing the club through with good hands-and-arms action.

Figure 2.6 The Long Iron. On long-iron shots, trigger the swing by making a powerful hip turn.

4. The Medium Iron
Play the ball near the middle of your stance. Swing to the three-quarter position on a slightly more upright angle than for a drive. Swing the club through with your arms.

5. The Short Iron
Assume a narrow open stance. (Try taking divots on the practice tee. Where the divot begins in relation to your feet is where you should play the ball.) Hit down on the ball.

Figure 2.7 The Pitching Wedge. Open the clubface and cock your wrists on the backswing before pulling the club down into the back of the ball.

6. The Pitching Wedge (Figure 2.7)
The pitching wedge should impart backspin. Assume an open stance. Play the ball a few inches in front of your back foot. Weaken your left hand. Hit down sharply.

7. The Pitch-and-Run
Plan to land the ball short of the green. Use a 7-iron. On the backswing, keep the club close to the ground and inside the target line.

8. The Chip (Figure 2.8)
Pick a spot on the green to land the ball. Assume a narrow open stance with most of your weight on your front foot. The open stance allows your hands to lead the club freely into the ball, making for a good nipping action at impact.

Figure 2.8 The Chip. On chips, pick the spot where you want the ball to land.

9. The Bunker Shot

Play the ball midway between your feet in an
open stance. Open the clubface of your sand
wedge. Cock your wrists on the backswing.
Unhinge your wrists on the downswing, and hit
down into the sand about 2 inches behind the
ball. (The wedge's bounce will prevent the club
from digging into the sand.)

10. The Putt

Position the ball opposite your left heel. Keep
your body and head still as you swing the
putterblade back and through low to the grass.
Use a pendulum-like, arms-shoulders action.

3 Ball-Control Shots

Here are four sophisticated variations on the basic shots:

BALL-CONTROL SHOTS AT A GLANCE

1. The Draw
2. The Fade

3. The Wind Cheater
4. The Texas Wedge

1. The Draw (Figure 3.1)
The draw (a slight, intentional hook) is used on doglegs, left to bring the ball around objects or

Figure 3.1 The Draw. Aim your body to the right of target.

to get a little more distance from overspin. To play a draw, close your stance, align your body to the right of the target but aim the clubface at the target. Swing normally. Note: If you still have trouble, strengthen your grip by turning both your hands away from the target.

2. The Fade (Figure 3.2)

A fade is a well-controlled slice. To play a fade, open your stance, aim your body to the left of the target but aim your clubface at the final target. Swing normally. If you still have a problem, weaken your grip by turning both of your hands toward the target.

Figure 3.2 The Fade. Aim your body to the left of target.

3. The Wind Cheater (The "Punch")

The punch is a hands and forearms shot hit into the green at a low trajectory ("under" the wind).

Set up as you would on a normal shot but use less body turn on your backswing. On the downswing make a quick transfer of your

58

weight to your front side. Use exaggerated rapid hand action and hit through crisply. (The hands must be in front of the clubface at impact.)

4. The Texas Wedge
(Figure 3.3)
This is a long putt. Use it when there are no hazards to carry and you can't get backspin on a chip because of a tight lie.

Stand as you would to play a driver, with your feet spread more than shoulder-width apart. This will encourage a low backswing. Lock your hips to promote a pure arms-shoulders stroke.

Swing the putterblade back low to the ground and through low to the ground. Take a longer backswing than you would for a putt, and hit the ball harder to allow for any slower fairway grass. This is a very easy shot to look up on, so keep your eyes fixed on the back of the ball.

Figure 3.3 The Texas Wedge. Widen stance and make an extended takeaway.

4 Situational Play

It would be nice if every time you hit the ball in the fairway you were guaranteed a nice flat lie with your ball sitting up. Unfortunately, topography, wind, weather, and less-than-perfect fairways make this not always the case. This chapter offers quick, simple instructions for hitting out of those not-so-unusual situations you encounter on the way to the hole.

SITUATIONAL PLAY AT A GLANCE

1. The Downhill Lie
2. The Uphill Lie
3. The Sidehill Lie (Ball Above Feet)
4. The Sidehill Lie (Ball Below Feet)
5. Chip Down a Steep Slope
6. Off Hardpan
7. Ball in Divot
8. Out of Clover
9. Out of Pine Needles
10. Ball on Fairway/ Rough Border
11. Ball in Thick Bermuda Grass Fringe
12. Headwind (on Drives)
13. Downwind (on Drives)
14. Left-to-Right Wind (on Approach Shots)
15. Right-to-Left Wind (on Approach Shots)
16. Wet Fairway
17. Plugged Lie
18. Fast Greens
19. Slow Greens
20. Wet Green (on Chips)
21. Wet Green (on Putts)

1. The Downhill Lie

Play the ball slightly closer than normal to your back foot. Assume an open stance. Bend your right knee inward for better balance. Since the ball tends to fly to the right off a downhill lie, aim left of the target (the steeper the slope the more you should aim to the left). Swing to the three-quarter position and use a controlled swing, mostly with your arms, as you come through the ball.

2. The Uphill Lie (Figure 4.1)

Your ball will fly higher than usual. Compensate by using one club longer (e.g., a 5-iron instead of a 6-iron). Use a square stance and play the ball in the middle of your feet. Address the ball with your body tilted back slightly to effectively give yourself a flat lie.

Prevent swaying on the backswing by minimizing your body turn. Generate clubhead speed by swinging mainly with your arms.

Figure 4.1 The Uphill Lie. Protect against loss of balance by exaggerated flexing of the forward knee.

3. The Sidehill Lie (Ball above Feet)
The ball will tend to hook off this lie, so compensate by aiming a little right of the target and slightly opening the clubface. Set your weight more on your toes. Take a controlled three-quarter backswing and try to sweep the ball off the grass.

4. The Sidehill Lie (Ball below Feet)
The ball will tend to fade off this lie. Compensate by aiming a little left of target and closing the clubface just a bit. Set your weight more on your heels.

Take a slow, compact swing and keep your head perfectly still. Looking up will cause a severe slice.

5. Chip Down a Steep Slope
Use a sand wedge. Open your stance and play the ball off your back foot.

Pick up the club quickly on your backswing, allowing your wrists to cock early in the takeaway. The action should feel very loose — "handsy."

On the downswing use your right hand to "drop" the club into the grass directly behind the ball.

6. Off Hardpan
When playing off hardpan aim slightly left of the target because the clubface opens at impact, yielding a left-to-right ball flight. Grip firmly with both hands to protect against the clubface opening violently at impact.

Hit down into the ball and generate high clubhead speed by making a strong upper body coil on the backswing and clearing your left hip quickly on the downswing.

7. Ball in Divot Hole
(Figure 4.2)
Set up for a very steep swing by playing the ball a couple of inches behind the midpoint of your stance. Place the majority of your weight on your front foot. Use a short, slow backswing, then replant your left heel at the start of the downswing and pull the club hard into the back of the ball.

Figure 4.2 Ball in Divot Hole. Replant your forward heel on the downswing.

8. Out of Clover
Clover will get between the ball and clubface at impact and your ball will fly up to 20 yards farther than usual. You should therefore use at least one club shorter than usual (e.g., a 7-iron instead of a 6-iron).

Make a smooth, compact backswing and shift your weight forward on the downswing, using your hands and arms to whip the club into the ball.

9. Out of Pine Needles

Brush away the pine needles where you intend to take your stance. Hover the clubhead above the needles directly behind the ball. (If you touch the needles the ball is likely to move and you may incur a penalty stroke.)

Assume your normal stance but balance your weight evenly on the balls of your feet.

Make a long takeaway away from the ball with the clubhead moving straight back along the target line. Swing up to the three-quarter position. Make a sweeping-type downswing so that the club comes into the ball – not the needles – squarely.

10. Ball on Fairway/Rough Border (Figure 4.3)

With the ball played midway between your feet,

Figure 4.3 Ball on Fairway/Rough Border. Take the club back outside the target line.

set up open to the target line. Aim to the left of the pin. Keep your knees flexed.

Take the club back steep and outside the target line on an out-to-in path. Flex your knees as you swing the club across the target line. This will put left-to-right spin on the ball and work it back to the hole.

11. Ball in Thick Bermuda Grass Fringe
In this situation the average golfer is often too quick to chip the ball with a short iron. A better choice of club is a putter. To play this shot, set up with the ball back in your stance but with more weight on your left foot.

Lift up the putterblade in the backswing by cocking your wrists quickly in the takeaway. Hit down on the ball to pop it out of the grass.

12. Headwind (on Drives)
Play the ball slightly back of your left heel. Swing back smoothly but on a flat plane. Maintain good rhythm and hit through the ball. Keep the clubhead moving low to the ground through impact and along the target line. Finish low.

13. Downwind (on Drives)
Play the ball forward in your stance. Hit a 3-wood and the ball will fly higher and ride the wind.

14. Left-to-Right Wind (on Approach Shots)
The strategy here is to use the wind to your advantage. Aim to the right of the flag. Swing the club on a flat plane and roll your right hand over your left through impact. The clubface will

turn over, imparting right-to-left spin on the ball. The ball will draw toward the target, meet the wall of wind blowing from the left, and drop down on target.

15. Right-to-Left Wind (on Approach Shots)
Aim left of the flag. Swing from outside to inside the target line and grip tightly with your left hand in the hitting area. The ball will fade into the wall of wind blowing from the right.

16. Wet Fairway
A wet fairway demands a sweeping action with the club to guard against hitting a fat shot. Play the ball off your front instep. Swing the club back on a shallow plane, keeping your hands closer to the ground. On the downswing, feel as if you are swinging out at the ball and sweep through it in the hitting area.

17. Plugged Lie
You're in luck. Local rules usually permit a free drop.

18. Fast Green
On a fast green don't shorten your stroke, or you will tend to decelerate the putter in the hitting zone and come up short of the hole. Use your normal putting stroke, but play the ball off the toe of the putter. This deadens the hit and allows for an "unconscious" adjustment to a fast green.

19. Slow Green
Purposefully strike the top half of the ball with the putterface. The overspin this imparts on the ball will compensate for slower-than-usual greens.

20. Wet Green (on Chips)
Don't run the ball to the hole; the surface water will slow your ball down. Play a wedge and plan on carrying the ball practically all the way to the hole.

21. Wet Green (on Putts)
Use your normal backstroke but focus on hitting the top portion of the ball; this will give you the overspin you need for reaching the hole.

5 Trouble Shots

For pros and amateurs alike, recovering from rough and hazards is as much a part of the game as hitting drives and putts, but these shots are among golf's toughest because they are encountered infrequently and for the average golfer practiced even more infrequently. This chapter offers the proper techniques for recovering from golf's most common situations.

TROUBLE SHOTS AT A GLANCE

1. Ball in Rough
2. Ball in Wet Rough
3. Shot over Trees
4. Shot Under Trees
5. Ball in Bunker, Feet Outside It
6. Powdery Sand
7. Coarse Sand
8. Ball Buried in Sand
9. Ball in "Fried Egg"
10. Fairway Bunker (Wood Shot)
11. Fairway Bunker (Iron Shot)
12. Ball in Bunker with No Lip
13. Ball Under Bush
14. Ball Half-Submerged in Water
15. Tree Prohibits Normal Stance and Swing
16. The Bank Shot
17. The Scurrier

1. Ball in Rough (Figure 5.1)

In rough, hit down more forcefully to pop the ball out of the heavy grass. To do this, use an open stance, play the ball farther back than you normally would, and place more weight on your front foot. Swing on a steeper-than-normal plane.

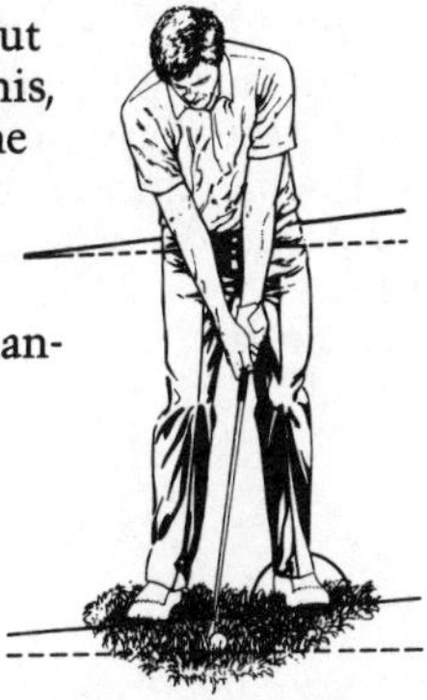

Figure 5.1 Ball in Rough. Place more weight on your forward foot and open your stance.

2. Ball in Wet Rough

Wet rough offers great resistance to the clubhead. To compensate, generate added clubhead speed by lightening your grip and whipping the club through.

Note: **The clubface will open slightly on impact, so close the face of the club when taking your stance.**

3. Shot over Trees (Figure 5.2)
This shot is largely mental. Start with a positive image of the ball flying over the trees. Play the ball off your left instep in a slightly open stance. Lay the clubface open. Take a full backswing, then keep your head behind the ball during the downswing. Pull the club through, using a loose, wristy action, and strive for a high finish.

Figure 5.2 Shot over Trees. Keep your head behind the ball through impact.

4. Shot Under Trees
Use a low iron. Take a square stance but play the ball farther back than usual. Set your hands ahead of the ball so the clubface is "hooded" (an exaggerated closing of the clubface). This will encourage a low trajectory.

Keep your weight to the front side on the backswing, and take a compact swing. On the downswing, keep the club moving low along the target line through impact.

5. Ball in Bunker, Feet Outside It (Figure 5.3)
Widen your stance about 6 inches for balance and crouch to bring your hands a natural distance from the ball. Keep your head and upper body still on the backswing. Hit down 2 inches behind the ball.

Figure 5.3 Ball in Bunker, Feet Outside It. Widen your stance to bring your hands within a natural distance of the ball.

6. Powdery Sand (Figure 5.4)

Hit farther behind the ball (about 3 inches) and let the sand wedge's natural bounce slide through the fine sand.

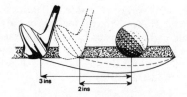

Figure 5.4   Powdery Sand. Hit 3 inches behind the ball.

7. Coarse Sand

Hit closer to the ball than usual, about 1 to 1½ inches.

8. Ball Buried in Sand

Use a pitching wedge, since its sharp leading edge will knife through the sand more effectively than a sand wedge. Assume a square but narrow stance and play the ball off your back foot. Hood the blade slightly. Pick the club up quickly by cocking your wrists during the takeaway and pull the club down through the sand, hitting about an inch before the ball.

The ball will come out "hot" so you might want to consider the "least worst" spot beyond the target for the ball to come to rest.

9. Ball in "Fried Egg"

If there is plenty of green to work with, play the shot just as you would for a ball buried in sand (See No. 8 above). If you must stop the ball quickly, assume an open stance, with the ball positioned off your back instep, and open the face of the sand wedge. Set your hands behind the ball and place most of your weight on your back foot. Bring the club back on an in-to-out swing path and, with a mostly hands-and-arms swing (little body action), pull the club down hard, contacting the sand 2 inches behind the ball.

10. Fairway Bunker (Wood Shot)
Open your stance and play the ball just off your front heel. Open the clubface slightly. Swing on an out-to-in path and allow for a slight fade.

11. Fairway Bunker (Iron Shot) (Figure 5.5)
Close your stance and play the ball in the middle. Close the clubface slightly. Swing on a flat plane and allow for a draw.

Figure 5.5 Fairway Bunker (Iron Shot). Swing the club on a flat plane.

12. Ball in Bunker with No Lip

Putt the ball. Swing the putterblade back low, using a dead-wristed swing. Contact the ball on the upswing, hitting firmly to compensate for the ball slowing down in the sand.

The following shots are for unusual situations that are rarely encountered. Be prepared nevertheless. Sacrifice some playing time to practice these shots by placing yourself in these awkward positions until you feel you "own" them.

13. Ball Under Bush (Figure 5.6)

For balls under shrubs or bushes, consider the "off-the-knees sweeper" before taking an unplayable lie.

Get down on your knees. Spread your knees wide apart so that you can make a good arm swing with no sway of the upper body. Stretch out both of your arms and set the club behind the ball. (This awkward setup will cause the

Figure 5.6   Ball under Bush. Swing the club on a shallow arc.

clubhead's sole to be a bit off the ground.
Compensate by closing the clubface.)

Keep your head still and swing the club back
and through on a shallow plane so that you
sweep through the ball.

14. Ball Half Submerged in Water
Use a sand wedge. Play the ball forward in your
stance to help you stay behind it at impact. Set
the majority of your weight on your front foot.
Open the clubface and hover it above the water,
2 inches behind the ball.

Swing the club on an out-to-in line and hit
twice as hard as you normally would (water
offers more resistance than it would seem).

15. Tree Prohibits Normal Stance and Swing (Figure 5.7)

When the ground is hard, a
putter shot played from your
opposite side (left-handed if
you are a right-handed player)
is the best strategy for hitting
the ball back to the fairway
or onto a green, from a
maximum distance of 25
yards.

Play the ball forward in a
wide stance and put more of
your weight on your back
foot to keep your body from
swaying.

Figure 5.7 Tree Prohibits Natural Stance and Swing. Swing
the putter back low.

Swing the putterblade back low and at a slow speed. Pull the putterblade through with your opposite hand leading.

16. The Bank Shot
(Figure 5.8)
When there is a grassy bank between your ball and the green (which is often the case when you fly the green), and there isn't much green to work with, the percentage shot may be a "bank"—a shot that hits into the bank, then bounces onto the green.

Analyze the grassy slope and visualize how the ball will react to the condition of the grass (the heavier the texture of the grass, the harder you must hit the ball). Pick the spot you want

Figure 5.8 The Bank Shot. Set this shot on "automatic pilot" by making a one-piece wristless takeaway.

to hit. Use a 7-iron when the bank is firm and the grass manicured, a 5-iron when the grass is soft or uncut. Play the ball in the middle of your stance but set your hands a couple of inches in front of the ball. Close the clubface slightly.

Take a slow backswing, keeping the club low to the ground and your wrists uncocked. Maintain the hands-ahead position through impact.

17. The "Scurrier"
(Figure 5.9)

The scurrier is a through-the-bunker shot that runs over the sand, through the fringe, and onto the green. It can be used when the trap is shallow and its lip is low. Use an 8-iron and, unless the ball is sitting down in heavy grass, use a normal chipping stroke. Focus on keeping your wrists stiff and lead the club into the ball with your hands.

Figure 5.9 The Scurrier. Let the hands lead the club into and through the impact zone.

6 Quick Fixes for Bad Shots

Golf is largely mental. When correcting a flaw in your golf swing the key is not simply understanding what you are doing wrong, but also knowing how to apply that knowledge. The secret to "applied golf knowledge" is to *think one key thought,* and only one key thought during your swing.

Obviously, the key thought may differ from shot to shot; the point is not to overwhelm your mind with five things you may be doing wrong on any one shot. Focus on what you believe is the key correction that needs to be made ("keep your head still," "slow down," etc.), and repeat it to yourself as you bring back the club.

Remember: *THINK ONE KEY THOUGHT.*

BAD SHOTS AT A GLANCE

1. The Push Slice
2. The Duck Hook
3. The Sky
4. The Top
5. The Shank
6. The Skull
7. The Pull
8. The Fat
9. The Thin
10. The Pulled Putt
11. The Pushed Putt

1. The Push Slice (Figure 6.1)

The push slice, which starts out right of the target and then flies farther right, is one of the most frustrating shots in golf.

There are dozens of causes for a slice, but the most common is cocking, or hinging, one's wrists too early in the takeaway. This, in turn, causes the player to flick his wrists at the beginning of the downswing. When that happens the club fails to meet the ball squarely at impact.

If you're a push slicer you can "quiet" your hand and wrist action by gripping more firmly with the last two fingers of your left hand and with the middle two fingers of your right hand. This will encourage a smoother one-piece takeaway. Using this grip, bring the club back low to the ground and inside the target line. If you are still having problems, close your stance and take a stronger grip by rolling your hands back on the club.

When all else fails aim left, but *square up* to the left-of-target point at which you are aiming. Otherwise, you will just slice more severely.

Figure 6.1 The Push Slice. To encourage an "anti-slice" takeaway, grip harder with the last two fingers of your left hand and with the middle two fingers of your right.

2. The Duck Hook. (Figure 6.2)

The Duck Hook starts left, flies farther left, and rolls with extra overspin. It is caused by coming across the ball or losing your balance during the swing. To counteract, *think hip turn*. Rotating your right hip during the backswing will improve tempo. Rotating your left hip on the downswing will "clear the hip" and discourage a baseball-swing type finish. A good hip rotation will also improve your balance.

Figure 6.2 The Duck Hook. To counteract, gently rotate your back hip on the backswing and forward hip on the downswing.

3. The Sky

Dipping the right shoulder at the start of the downswing is the major cause of skying the ball. And dipping is caused by using too much right hand on the downswing. Compensate by focusing on leading more with your left hand — pulling the club through with your left rather than *forcing* it down with your right.

4. The Top

Falling back on your heels, thus hitting the ball above its center, is the chief cause of topping the ball. To compensate, bend more at the knees and the waist. This will shift your weight toward the ball and encourage proper balance.

5. The Shank (Figure 6.3)

The shank is caused by unintentionally lining up the clubface well right of the target, thus creating impact with the ball near the club's hosel rather than on the sweet spot. To cure it, focus on "squaring" your setup with feet, knees, hips, and shoulders parallel to an imaginary line that runs through the center of the ball to the target. The clubface should be perpendicular, or "square," to this imaginary line.

Figure 6.3 The Shank. To cure "the shanks," a square setup encourages a square impact.

6. The Skull
The skull is a modified airborne top, with the ball taking off, uncontrolled, at a low trajectory. It is generally caused by flicking at the ball (much as a fisherman might flick a rod) at the top of the downswing. Focus on stiffening your left arm and wrist and pulling the club into the ball with your left hand. This will encourage a less "wristy" shot. Alternatively, concentrate on firmly planting your left heel on the downswing. This exaggerated weight shift will also make for a more left-sided shot.

7. The Pull
Playing the ball too far forward in your stance will cause the ball to fly on a line left of the target. To compensate, try playing the ball slightly farther back than you normally would. On a drive, for example, play the ball opposite your left heel, or even 1 or 2 inches farther back.

8. The Fat
Swinging the club back on a plane that is too upright causes you to hit the ball fat. To cure, focus on rotating your shoulders as you bring back the club. This will help bring the club back inside the target line and on a much flatter plane, making for a nipping rather than chopping action at impact.

9. The Thin
Hitting the ball thin, or on the toe of the club, is often caused by attempting to swing the club on an in-to-out path and *throwing* the clubhead into the ball (rather than *swinging* through it).

To cure, focus on driving your right shoulder under your chin on the downswing and through the hitting area.

10. The Pulled Putt
Pulled putts are usually caused by having the right hand take over on the downswing. To cure, straighten your left arm at address, stiffen your wrist, and grip a little firmer with your left hand. This will discourage your right hand from taking over. Keep your head still and focus on using the stiff left hand to hit *through* the ball. (Don't quit on the shot.)

11. The Pushed Putt
(Figure 6.4)
Improper alignment is often the cause of a pushed putt: the ball rolls to the right of the target because your shoulders are aimed to the right of the target. At address, recheck to make sure your body, especially your shoulders, are aligned squarely to the ball. Also make sure your head is directly over the ball.

Figure 6.4 The Pushed Putt. To cure, set your body parallel to the ball, with your head directly over the ball.

7 Quick Fixes for Common Ailments

The golf swing may be the most unnatural physical action in all of sport. As a result it is more likely to break down than an old car. Fortunately, when it does break down the ailment is likely to be a common one. Whatever ailment you figure is affecting your golf game is probably treated in this chapter.

COMMON AILMENTS AT A GLANCE

1. Looking Up
2. Incorrect Weight Shift
3. Coming off the Ball
4. Bending the Left Arm
5. Swinging Too Fast
6. Pulling the Ball (on Drives)
7. Pushing the Ball (on Short Irons)
8. Hitting the Wrong Club
9. Hitting Chips Heavy
10. No Spin
11. Can't Get the Ball over High Bunker Lip
12. Can't Read Green
13. "Yips" On Short Putts
14. When the Wheels Come Off

1. Looking Up
Fix your eyes on a single point on the back of the ball. Excessively flex your knees as you set up to the ball. (This adjustment will improve your balance on the downswing so that you can keep your head steady at impact.)

2. Incorrect Weight Shift (Figure 7.1)
Nothing disrupts the rhythm and tempo of a golf swing more than an incorrect weight shift, also known as a reverse pivot.

In a sound swing a player's weight shifts heavily to his rear foot on the upswing and then shifts back to his front foot (and side) on the downswing. With the reverse pivot a golfer's

Figure 7.1 Incorrect Weight Shift. To help you shift your weight correctly to your right foot on the backswing, rotate your left knee inward.

weight is on the front foot on the backswing and the back foot on the downswing. To cure, rotate your front knee inward (away from the target) as you start the swing. This will help shift your weight to the rear side on the upswing and encourage proper weight shift on the downswing.

3. Coming off the Ball
The player who comes off the ball has his club in an open rather than square position at impact. To promote "squareness," imagine a second ball you also want to hit is 6 inches in front of your real ball. This will encourage you to swing through the ball at impact.

4. Bending the Left Arm
(Figure 7.2)
Set up so that your left arm
and the clubshaft form a
straight line. Focus on
dragging the clubhead
straight back along the target
line for a distance of 12
inches.

Figure 7.2 Bending the Left Arm. To cure, make sure the club and your front arm form a straight line.

5. Swinging Too Fast

Players usually swing too fast because they yank back the club. First, slow down for the first 12 inches. Then, concentrate on swinging the triangle formed by your arms and shoulders back as one unified piece. This will prevent you from getting too handsy, which will automatically improve your tempo.

6. Pulling the Ball (on Drives)

You may be playing the ball too far forward in your stance. Play the ball opposite your left heel.

7. Pushing the Ball (on Short Irons)

You may be playing the ball too far back off your back foot. Move the ball up in your stance, no farther than the midpoint.

8. Hitting the Wrong Club

Don't hit a shot until you know where the 150-yard marker is. Check the wind by tossing blades of grass in the air. More important, check which way and how hard the wind is blowing at the top of any trees. On uphill shots allow for an additional 10 to 20 yards, on downhill shots subtract 10 yards. The Golden Rule: When in doubt take the stronger club since there is usually less trouble behind a green.

9. Hitting Chips Heavy

Fat chips are usually caused by making a stroke that is too handsy. Keep your wrists firm and lead the club into the ball with your hands, not your wrists.

10. No Spin
To impart backspin set up with the ball slightly behind the midpoint in your stance. This will give you a more upright swing and more nipping action at impact.

11. Can't Get the Ball over High Bunker Lip (Figure 7.3)
Open the clubface more than usual. Make an exaggerated upright, wristy backswing, then uncock the wrists and slap the sand with the sole of the club about 2 inches behind the ball.

Figure 7.3 Can't Get the Ball over High Bunker Lip. Exaggerate the wrist action and slap the sand with the club.

12. Can't Read Green
First check the overall lay of the land. Is the course laid out near mountains or a large body of water? Assume the ball will break down the mountain or toward the nearest body of water before adjusting for the lay of the green. Whenever confused by the break, allow for less break rather than more.

13. "Yips" on Short Putts
Visualize a backstop behind the hole to promote a firm putting stroke.

14. When the Wheels Come Off

Visualize a good shot. Replay good shots from a past round in your mind, or see in your mind one of the top pros hitting the same shot. Take three deep breaths. (Even the pros do it.) Close your eyes while making a practice swing to get a good feel for the swing. Grip lightly for better clubhead feel.

8 Trick Shots

When all else fails, here are three shots that may distract your partners from how badly you are playing.

1. The Rocket Shot

This trick shot is actually easier than it sounds. First, on the ground, stack one golf ball on top of another. (This will take some patience but it can be done.) Then, using a middle iron (it will also work with a wood) take your natural swing at the bottom ball. It will fly down the fairway while the top ball will shoot straight up into the air. (You'll really amaze your friends if you can learn to catch the falling ball in your back pocket!)

2. The Over-the-Shoulder Putt

You'll need a Ping-type putter that features a cavity behind the putterface. Stand on a green with your back turned to the hole 20 feet away. Scoop up the ball in the putter's cavity and continue swinging the club over your head, as if you were making a basketball hook shot. With a little practice, you'll develop enough feel so that the ball will roll near the hole every time.

3. The Sleeve Shot

Empty two of the three balls from a new sleeve of golf balls. Stand the sleeve upright on the grass with the remaining ball at the bottom. With a long or middle iron swing hard at the bottom of the box. The force of impact will send the ball flying out of the box and a good distance down the fairway.

9 Handicapping and Scorekeeping

The handicap is the great equalizer in golf, allowing players of different calibers to play evenly. Handicaps are normally calculated/distributed by regional golf associations. But you can also calculate your own. All you need is the same information a player must provide to the golf association: (1) your scores; (2) the course rating of the course on which you played; and (3) the "Slope rating" of the course.

> *Note:* **A handicap you calculate yourself cannot be used in competition. It will not be an official "USGA Handicap."**

A course rating refers to the score a scratch golfer — one whose handicap is zero — would shoot on the course. It is expressed to a decimal point and is based on yardage and other standardized factors.

A Slope rating refers to a course's *relative* difficulty for average players compared to expert players. It dawned on the USGA a few years ago that not only would less-skilled golfers encounter more trouble on a difficult course, they would also take, on average, more strokes to recover. In other words, the tougher the course, the greater the discrepancy between the skilled and the unskilled golfer. The USGA then created a system of rating a course to indicate its relative difficulty. A course of average difficulty is assigned a Slope rating of 113.

Anything above that is considered tougher than normal; anything below easier than normal.

The regional organizations then began to issue golfers "handicap *indexes*" instead of handicaps. The golfer takes his index, also expressed to a decimal point, to any golf course, whereupon he checks the course's Slope rating (it is posted on a Course Handicap Table in either the pro shop or the locker room) and finds out what his handicap will be for that course. If, for example, a golfer has a handicap index of 12.0 and he is about to play a course with a Slope rating of 135 (difficult), he will likely play with a handicap of 13 or 14 that day. If the Slope rating is low, he will play off a lower number—10 or 11 perhaps.

Calculate Your Own Index

First calculate the handicap differential of each round you play. The differential is calculated by subtracting the course rating from your score once it has had "Equitable Stroke Control" applied (see below). You then multiply that number by 113 (the average Slope rating) and divide that number by the course's Slope rating.

For example, suppose you shoot a 90 (adjusted) on a course that has a course rating of 71.5 and a Slope rating of 125. Subtract 71.5 from 90 (90 − 71.5 = 18.5) and multiply 18.5 by 113 (18.5 × 113 = 2090). Divide 2090 by the Slope rating of 125 (2090 ÷ 125 = 16.7). Your handicap differential is 16.7. The final calculation involves multiplying the average of the ten lowest handicap differentials from your twenty most recent rounds by 96 percent. If you

have not played twenty rounds (the minimum
requirement is five rounds), follow this table:

5 or 6 rounds	1 lowest differential
7 or 8 rounds	2 lowest differentials
9 or 10 rounds	3 lowest differentials
11 or 12 rounds	4 lowest differentials
13 or 14 rounds	5 lowest differentials
15 or 16 rounds	6 lowest differentials
17 rounds	7 lowest differentials
18 rounds	8 lowest differentials
19 rounds	9 lowest differentials

Another example: Suppose you have an
average handicap differential (total of 10 lowest
handicap differentials divided by 10) of 17.2.
Then, 17.2 × 96 percent = 16.5. Your handicap
index is 16.5.

Equitable Stroke Control

To prevent a couple of really bad holes from
drastically affecting a player's handicap, the
USGA has also created what is known as
"Equitable Stroke Control," which details how a
player should adjust his score for *handicapping
purposes only*.

With a course handicap of:

0	A player cannot take more than 1 over par on more than 1 hole.
1–18	A player cannot take more than 2 over par on the number of holes equal to his course handicap (e.g., for a course handicap of 8, no more than 8 holes). He cannot take more than 1 over par on the remaining holes.

| 19–36 | A player cannot take more than 3 over par on the number of holes his course handicap exceeds 18 (e.g., for a course handicap of 25 a limit of 7 holes). He cannot take more than 2 over par on the remaining holes. |
| 37–40 | A player cannot take more than 4 over par on the number of holes his course handicap exceeds 36 (e.g., with a course handicap of 40, no more than 4 holes). He cannot take more than 3 over par on the remaining holes. |

TO GET AN OFFICIAL HANDICAP

An official USGA Handicap is one that is issued via a regional golf association and can only be obtained if you belong to a club. But if you do not belong to a club with five-figure membership fees, fear not. One of the newest and fastest-growing segments in the world of golf involves "clubs-on-wheels."

They work like this: A club can comprise any group of ten or more golfers who, according to the USGA: (1) have "a reasonable and regular opportunity to play golf with each other and must be able personally to return their scores"; (2) have "peer review" (in other words, they must form a committee to supervise and scrutinize play), and (3) they must have a set of bylaws. That's not tough. The USGA is happy

to mail off literature titled "Bylaws for Golf
Clubs Without Real Estate."

Most clubs keep forms for posting adjusted
scores in the locker room (or an office, if your
club is one formed with workmates). You can
use this model to calculate and record your own
scores and either enter them at your leisure, or
calculate your own, unofficial handicap.

DATE SCORE COURSE RATING SLOPE RATING DIFFERENTIAL

_____

_____

_____

_____

_____

_____

_____

_____

_____

_____

_____

SCOREKEEPING (NOT FOR HANDICAPPING PURPOSES)

There is a simple way to keep score in your
head. Keep a running under/over tally as you go,
but rather than "even" being par, assume that
"even" represents a score of all fours (for an
"even par" of 72), all fives (for an "even par" of
90), and all sixes (for an "even par" of 108),
depending on your level of skill.

In other words, if you play to around 90, add or subtract strokes from 5 on every hole. For example, if your scores on the first nine holes are 4, 4, 6, 5, 3, 5, 4, 5, 6, you would be "three under fives" for a nine-hole total of 42.

10 Games and Bets

Few golfers play a round without playing some
sort of game. The most popular is the "Nassau,"
in which a set amount of money is bet on the
front nine holes, the back nine, and the overall
round. But there are many more games a group
can play. What follows are twenty games that
are easy to learn and play. None has to be played
for particularly high stakes or, for that matter,
any money at all.

Note: **When you are playing a game that might
involve extra scorekeeping, or present unusual
situations, do not delay play for the other golfers
on the course.**

1. Bingle, Bangle, Bungle
Three points are up for grabs. One goes to the
player reaching the green first. The second goes
to whoever is closest to the hole when all the
balls in the group are on the green. The third
goes to whoever holes his ball first. The winner
is the player with the most points at the end of
the round.

2. Flag Day
Each player is given a small flag or similar
marker. When he has hit the same number of
shots as par for the course plus his handicap, he
sticks the flag in the ground. The winner is the
player who carries the flag farthest around the
course.

3. Four of Clubs

This is a fun game that will help your shot-making. Put simply, players must play with only four clubs and improvise many shots. A player might choose, for example, a driver, a 6-iron, a wedge, and a putter. It is up to the player to know how many different shots he can hit.

In a variation, the number of clubs carried varies according to the relative skills of the players.

4. High Score

This is a good game to play in a threesome. Each hole is worth 12 points. Low score wins 6 points, second score 4, and third score 2. If scores are equal, the players divide the points. Players can choose their own values for each hole, but they should ensure that the tallies can be divided by 2 or 3, should holes be halved.

5. Long Shots

Instead of a player winning a hole with the best score, he wins the yardage of the hole. Whoever wins the most yards by the end of the day wins the match.

6. Low Total

In a normal four-ball match, players play "better ball," in which the best score wins the hole for that side. In "Low Total," however, low score wins 1 point and the low total for the hole also wins 1 point. This keeps players who would otherwise be out of the hole involved.

A variation awards 1 point for low ball, and a second point for the lower of the two higher scores.

7. Nassau
The most common golf bet involves wagering a set amount (usually $2–$5) on the front nine holes, the back nine, and the full eighteen. If a player, or a side, wins the front, he collects $2. If he wins the front and the back and, obviously, the full eighteen, he collects $6. If any of the bets are halved, no money changes hands.

8. Play It Again, Sam
Instead of the lesser player being awarded handicap strokes, the better player must, at the request of the opponent, replay certain shots. Say, for example, that a 12 handicapper is playing an 8 handicapper. He might force the better player to replay four shots. This can get very interesting if the opportunities are used wisely, such as to force the replay of a great putt or a successful trouble shot.

9. Press
A press bet can be used in any game but is mostly used to make Nassau interesting. A player can "press" at any time when he wants to make a new bet. If, for instance, he is two holes down with two to play, he can announce that he'll press, and the bet is for the two remaining holes only. The catch is that the stakes are doubled. A player can keep pressing to create new bets—probably to try to retrieve some of his losses—but the stakes double each time.

There are two other kinds of press: an "automatic press" means a player has to press when he is a set amount of holes behind, and an "aloha press," which is a bet a player will make with one hole remaining if he is in danger of losing all three ways. Let's say, for instance, that he owes $2 for the front nine, $2 for the eighteen, and is likely to lose the back nine, too. He can call an "aloha press" on the last hole. If he wins the hole, he ends up even. If he halves the hole, he loses what he would have lost anyway. But if he loses this hole, too, then he has to pay double.

10. Scramble
This is a popular format for tournaments, but can also be used in everyday play. When each player on a side has teed off, the side chooses the best shot, and each player then hits from there. One version of the scramble has players alternating shots once they are on the green.

11. Short Putts
This is a game that discourages tentative putting. A player must ante up a set amount to his opponents whenever he leaves short a putt for par or better.

12. Skins
This already popular game has become even more popular with the advent of the annually televised "Skins Game."

Players agree to a certain dollar amount for each "skin." A player wins a skin by winning a hole outright. If no one wins the hole, the skin is carried over and the next hole is worth two skins, and so on.

In some variations the value of the skins increases as the round goes on.

13. The Worst of Two
Each player takes a turn at playing against the *worst* score in the rest of the group. Say, for example, that the player shoots a 5 while his three opponents shoot 4, 5, and 6; he would win the hole by virtue of his 5 beating the 6.

14. Snake
This is a game that preys on poor putters. The first player to three-putt is said to be holding the snake. He continues to hold it until another player three-putts. Whoever is holding the snake at the end of the round—i.e., the last to three-putt—must pay either a set amount to the other players in the group, or buy drinks, dinner, etc.

15. Six-Six-Six
This game allows a foursome of two teams to play three different games within one round. The team members alternate shots for six holes; the players play their own balls for another six holes; and the players scramble (with each team hitting from the spot of their team's best shot) for the last six holes.

16. Stableford
This is a popular tournament format in which point values are assigned to scores. In the most common version, bogey is worth 1 point, par is worth 2, birdie 3, and eagle 4. But players can also adjust point values according to their level of play.

17. String
In a string tournament, each player is given a set length of string and a pair of scissors. The

player can move his ball anywhere on the course, but has to cut off a length of string equal to the distance he moved his ball. Let's say a player starts with 8 feet of string. If he moves his ball 3 feet to escape a water hazard, he is left with 5 feet of string. If he is then facing a dicey 3-foot putt, he can claim it as holed and cut off another 3 feet. The strategy is knowing how to best use your string.

18. Trash

This game normally includes what are known as "greenies" or "sandies." A player wins a monetary unit (normally a quarter) each time he hits a par-three green with his tee shot. He also wins a unit when he gets up and down from a bunker in two shots (some groups only pay for sandies that result in par or better).

Trash can also be expanded to include:

Arnie: Player misses fairway *and* green, but makes par (as Arnld Palmer would do)

Barkie: Ball hits tree — but only if loud enough to be heard — and player makes par

Gigglie: Player's mishit makes opponent laugh — but he still makes par

Gurglie: Ball goes into water, but player makes par

Hogie: Routine par, fairway hit, green hit, two putts (as Ben Hogan would do)

Offie: Anything holed from off the green

19. Vegas

You'll need a pencil and paper to keep track of this game, but it is fun. A side's score for a hole is determined by each player's performance on the hole. Say, for example, that one partner scores a 4 and the other a 5. Their score would be 45 (the low number goes first). If the other side shoots a 5 and a 6, for a 56, the first side would be up by 11. In addition, if someone shoots a birdie the other team has to reverse its scores. If the team shooting birdie, for example, goes 2-4 and the other side goes 3-6, that would mean scores of a 24 and a 63, for a differential on the hole of 39.

20. Wolf

There are many variations to this game. The most common involves each player taking his turn at being the "wolf," and choosing a partner at each hole after everyone has teed off. The hole is then played as a low-ball game.

Some players make the wolf either pick his partner or "pass" after each tee shot. Another variation has a player able to pass on everyone and take the rest of the group on by himself. If he chooses to do that, the bets are doubled.

MAKE UP YOUR OWN GAMES

Golfers can always make up their own games. A less-skilled player, for example, might be allowed a certain amount of mulligans (do-overs) during the round. Another popular game involves one player electing how each hole should be played. One player might demand that a par 5 be played only with 9-irons, while another player might demand that a very short hole be played only with drivers. Some tournaments take this idea even further, organizing one-club tournaments in which a player can carry, as the name suggests, only one club.

It all depends on the golfer's imagination.

11 A Golf Glossary.

Ace   A hole in one.
Address   The position assumed when ready to hit.
Albatross Score of 2 under par on a hole; also known as "double eagle.".
Approach   A shot played toward a green.
Apron   Short grass around the putting green.
Away   A golfer is away when he is farthest from the hole and it is his turn to play

Birdie   Score of 1 under par on a hole.
Bite   Backspin on a ball that makes it stop sharply.
Blade   Type of putter on which the shaft is connected to the head at the heel. Can also mean a topped shot in which the leading edge of the club hits the ball first.
Blind hole A hole on which the landing area cannot be seen from the hitting area.
Bogey   Score of 1 over par on a hole.

Caddie   The person who carries a player's clubs and advises him on how to play a course.
Carry   The distance a ball travels between impact and landing.
Chip shot A short approach shot.
Choke down To hold the club down the grip.
Cleek   Old name for a 4-wood.
Closed stance Stance with the right foot drawn back from a line parallel to the target line, the left foot on the line.
Cross bunker A sandtrap normally positioned perpendicular to the direction of a hole.
Cut shot   Normally a short, high shot hit by bringing the club across the ball from out to in.

Divot	Turf dug out by a club during a swing.
Dogleg	The shape of a hole that curves right or left.
Dormie	Situation in match play when a player is ahead by the amount of holes remaining.
Double bogey	Score of 2 over par on a hole.
Double eagle	Score of 3 under par on a hole.
Draw	A controlled shot that curves from right to left
Eagle	Score of 2 under par on a hole.
Explosion	A short sand shot that digs up a lot of sand and resembles an explosion
Fade	A controlled shot that curves from left to right.
Fairway	The closely mown part of the golf course between the teeing ground and the green.
Fat	Description of a mishit in which the club digs in well behind the ball.
Flange	The heavy base of a sand wedge that keeps it from digging into sand.
Flat	Description of swing in which the club is swung around the torso. Also refers to an obtuse angle between a clubhead and shaft.
Follow-through	The completion of the swing after impact.
Fore!	What to shout when a ball might hit someone.
Fourball	A group of four golfers each playing one ball.
Foursome	A group of four golfers in which teams of two alternate shots with one ball.

Fried egg A partially buried lie in a bunker resembling a fried egg.

Fringe Short grass around a green

Gimme A putt so short it does not have to be putted.

Grain The direction grass grows on a green.

Green fee The fee paid to play golf.

Gross score Total strokes taken, including penalty strokes.

Ground under repair Ground marked as temporarily unfit for play.

Handicap The number with which a player adjusts his score to reflect his playing ability.

Hanging lie A stance where the ball lies below a player's feet.

Heel The point where the back of the clubhead meets the shaft.

Hole in one A score of 1 on a hole.

Honor The right to tee off first.

Hood To tilt the clubhead forward (to hit a low shot) while keeping the clubface square to the target line.

Hook An uncontrolled shot that flies right to left.

Hosel Where the shaft is inserted into the clubhead.

Insert The part of a wood's clubface that can be replaced or repaired.

Inside the leather A putt closer to the hole than the distance between a putter's head and its grip.

Lag	A long putt hit to leave an easy, short putt.
Lie	Where a ball comes to rest.
Line	The direction a ball must travel to reach the hole.
Links	A seaside course found normally on dune land that "links" the sea to the mainland.
Lip	The rim of the hole.
Lob	A high shot that lands softly.
Loft	The angle of a clubface.
LPGA	Ladies Professional Golf Association.
Mulligan	A replayed shot hit normally after a poor tee shot. It is a casual arrangement.
Nassau	A three-part bet in which golfers vie for the front nine, the back nine, and the whole round.
Net score	The score after handicap strokes are subtracted.
NGF	National Golf Foundation.
Open stance	A stance with the left foot set back from a line parallel to the target line, the right foot on the line.
Par	The number of strokes a skilled player should take on a hole.
Penalty stroke	An extra stroke incurred for violating a rule or taking relief from a hazard or unplayable lie.
PGA of America	Professional Golfers' Association of America, an association of club professionals.
PGA Tour	The association for touring professionals.
Pin	The flagstick.

Pitch	A short, high approach that stops quickly.
Pitch and run	A pitch that rolls to the hole.
Pitching wedge	A club used to hit short approaches.
Play through	To overtake a slower or larger group.
Plugged lie	A ball embedded in the ground.
Pot bunker	A small, deep sandtrap.
Pull	A mishit that flies directly left.
Punch	A hard, low shot normally hit in windy conditions.
Push	A mishit that flies directly right
Rough	Long grass on the golf course.
Rub of the green	A golfing term for a stroke of normally bad luck.
Run up	An approach shot that bounces and rolls toward the hole.
Sandbagger	A skilled golfer who claims to be unskilled to gain a competitive edge.
Sandtrap	A hazard filled with sand.
Sand wedge	An iron with a thick sole used predominantly in sandtraps.
Scratch player	A golfer whose handicap is zero.
Shaft	The part of the club that connects the head and the grip.
Shank	A severe mishit in which the ball is struck by the hosel and squirts right.
Skull	To hit the top of the ball with the leading edge of the club.
Sky	A pop-up.

Slice	An uncontrolled shot that flies left to right.
Sole	The bottom of the clubhead.
Soleplate	A metal plate on the bottom of a wooden club.
Spoon	Old name for a 3-wood.
Square	A match that is even. A "square stance" has both feet on a line parallel to the target line.
Stance	The position of the feet at address.
Stymied	To have any form of obstruction between your ball and the target.
Sweet spot	The part of the clubface that imparts the best contact with the ball.
Takeaway	The start of the backswing.
Tee	The implement on which you place a ball for a tee shot.
Texas wedge	Term for a putter when used from off the green.
Toe	The outer part of the clubface.
Top	A mishit where a player hits the top of the ball.
Underclub	To use a club that won't hit the required distance.
Upright swing	A swing in which the club is swung high above the shoulders.
Waggle	The flexing of the clubhead before the swing.
Wedge	A short iron with a heavy sole.
Whiff	To miss the ball completely.
Whipping	Twine used to secure the head of a wooden club to the shaft.
Yips	An affliction in which a golfer's nerves cause the hands and arms to twitch while putting.

12 Equipment Care

Woods

Wooden clubs should always be covered by head covers.

If the insert in the face of the club is screwed into the head, it is a good idea to check periodically that the screws are all tight. Apart from preventing the insert from coming off, this will help you hit your shots with full impact. Regularly and often you should wash your woods in warm, lightly soapy water with a soft-bristle brush, then towel dry. If your woods do become chipped, take them to your club professional or a club-repair professional for refinishing. Metal woods should be treated as irons (below).

Irons

Moisture is your irons' worst enemy, as most are made of stainless steel and are vulnerable to rust. Wash your clubs regularly in warm, soapy water and scrub with a soft-bristle brush, then towel dry. It is also a good idea to give them the occasional coat of rust preventative.

If you intend to store your clubs for a long time—in the winter, for example—it is a good idea to give them a light coating of oil. Any oil, even motor oil, will do. This prevents any moisture from gathering. You do not need to coat your woods, as they normally have a

coating (the most common being polyurethane).
Your shafts will most likely be chrome plated
and will not require an application of oil.

Grips

It is surprising how rarely amateur golfers
change their grips, particularly since a good,
firm grip is such an integral part of the swing.
Of course, how often you change your grips
depends on how often you play, but a good rule
of thumb is once a year. The cost ranges from
$2.50 to $6 per club, depending on the type of
grip you want (rubber, cord, rubber/cord, or
leather), and who is performing the task.

A good way to prolong the life of your grip is
to wash and dry the grips, then rub them gently
with a fine grade of sandpaper. Wash your grips
regularly in warm soapy water with a soft brush
and towel dry. (This will remove the grease that
came from your hands.)

SHOES

Golf shoes should have the dirt scraped from
the cleats with a wire brush. To dry wet golf
shoes, insert wooden shoe trees and let them
dry naturally.

It is not necessary to treat leather golf shoes
with any special cream or polish, as regular
shoe polish will do. Never leave wet golf shoes
in a damp area for any length of time.

GLOVES

It is a good idea to invest in "glove trees," artificial hands made from plastic or metal that allow gloves to be stretched to their normal size as they dry out. It is possible to apply leather conditioner, but golf gloves gather so much grease and dirt and rain that it is often easier to invest in new gloves.

13 Course Notes

The following pages will allow you to keep
personalized notes on how to best play the most
challenging (or troublesome) holes on your
favorite courses. You should use it to jot down
reminders about how best to play each hole.

COURSE: _____

HOLE:_____ PAR:_____ YARDS:_____

_____

_____

_____

_____

_____

HOLE:_____ PAR:_____ YARDS:_____

_____

_____

_____

_____

_____

Course Notes

COURSE: _____

HOLE:_____ PAR:_____ YARDS:_____

_____

_____

_____

_____

_____

_____

_____

HOLE:_____ PAR:_____ YARDS:_____

_____

_____

_____

_____

_____

_____

_____

Course Notes

COURSE: _____

HOLE:_____ PAR:_____ YARDS:_____

_____

_____

_____

_____

_____

_____

_____

HOLE:_____ PAR:_____ YARDS:_____

_____

_____

_____

_____

_____

_____

_____

Course Notes

COURSE: _____

HOLE:_____ PAR:_____ YARDS:_____

_____

_____

_____

_____

_____

_____

_____

HOLE:_____ PAR:_____ YARDS:_____

_____

_____

_____

_____

_____

_____

_____

Course Notes

COURSE: _____

HOLE:_____ PAR:_____ YARDS:_____

_____

_____

_____

_____

_____

_____

_____

HOLE:_____ PAR:_____ YARDS:_____

_____

_____

_____

_____

_____

_____

_____

Course Notes

COURSE: _____

HOLE:_____ PAR:_____ YARDS:_____

_____

_____

_____

_____

_____

_____

_____

HOLE:_____ PAR:_____ YARDS:_____

_____

_____

_____

_____

_____

_____

_____

Course Notes

COURSE: _____

HOLE:_____ PAR:_____ YARDS:_____

_____

_____

_____

_____

_____

_____

_____

HOLE:_____ PAR:_____ YARDS:_____

_____

_____

_____

_____

_____

_____

_____

Course Notes

COURSE: _____

HOLE:_____ PAR:_____ YARDS:_____

_____

_____

_____

_____

_____

_____

_____

HOLE:_____ PAR:_____ YARDS:_____

_____

_____

_____

_____

_____

_____

_____

Course Notes

COURSE: _____

HOLE:_____ PAR:_____ YARDS:_____

_____

_____

_____

_____

_____

_____

_____

HOLE:_____ PAR:_____ YARDS:_____

_____

_____

_____

_____

_____

_____

_____

Course Notes

COURSE: _____

HOLE: _____ PAR: _____ YARDS: _____

_____

_____

_____

_____

_____

_____

_____

HOLE: _____ PAR: _____ YARDS: _____

_____

_____

_____

_____

_____

_____

_____

14 The Magnificent Obsession

Three Ultimate Golf Jokes about the Grip of the Game:

- A man returning from a day's golf is greeted by his wife, who comments on how drained he looks.

  "Yeah, it was a real tough day," the husband replies. "You wouldn't believe it. We were standing on the second tee when Harry has a heart attack, keels over, and dies!"

  "That must have been awful," the wife replies.

  "You're telling me," said the husband. "For the rest of the round it was 'Hit the ball, drag Harry . . . hit the ball, drag Harry . . . hit the ball, drag Harry . . .'"

- An avid golfer was on a cruise when the ship sank. The ship's only survivor, he managed to swim to a desert island.

  After several weeks of no signs of life, he was awakened one morning by a beautiful young lady walking out of the sea wearing only a skin-tight wetsuit.

  "You must be hungry," she said to the castaway golfer as she stroked his hair.

  "S-s-starving," he replied, at which point she unzipped the top of her wetsuit and pulled out some cheese and some French bread.

  "Thirsty?" she said as the golfer tucked away the food.

"V-v-very," he said, at which point she went into her wetsuit again and pulled out a cold beer.

"Like a smoke?" she asked next.

"L-l-love one," said the man as he drained the beer.

"Now," she said leaning close to him. "I suppose you'd like to play around . . ."

"Wow!" exclaimed the man. "You've got a set of golf clubs in there, too?"

- A quartet of golfers is playing a hole that involves crossing a road. As they approach the road, a hearse drives by, followed by a long cavalcade of cars.

  As the cortège drives slowly by, one of the golfers takes his hat off and bows his head.

  "I didn't know you were that respectful of the dead," remarked another in the group when the funeral procession had passed.

  "Well," said the first golfer. "We were married for twenty-seven years."

Robin McMillan is the Editor of Golf Magazine Custom Publishing, and was previously *GOLF Magazine*'s Senior Editor in charge of news and features. He is the author of several golf books, including *The Golfer's Home Companion, 365 One-Minute Golf Lessons: Quick and Easy Stroke-Saving Tips and Exercises,* as well as coeditor with George Peper of *Golf in America: The First One Hundred Years.*

John Andrisani has coauthored numerous instructional books with some of the world's top golfers and golf instructors, including *Learning Golf: The Lyle Way* with Sandy Lyle, *Natural Golf* with Seve Ballesteros, *Total Shotmaking* with Fred Couples, and *The Four Cornerstones of Winning Golf* with Claude "Butch" Harmon Jr. He is a regular contributor to golf magazines worldwide, and has won the American Golf Writer's Championship. He was formerly a golf instructor and was a Senior Instructional Editor of *GOLF Magazine.*

Ken Lewis lives in England, and is one of the foremost golf illustrators in the world.